ROCKS: The Hard Facts

EARTH'S ROCK CYCLE

Willa Dee

PowerKiDS press.

New York

Published in 2014 by The Rosen Publishing Group, Inc.
29 East 21st Street, New York, NY 10010

First Edition

Editor: Jennifer Way
Book Design: Kate Vlachos
Photo Research: Katie Stryker

Photo Credits: Cover Alfredo Cerra/Shutterstock.com; p. 5 Nerdist72/Shutterstock.com; p. 6 Lukiyanova Natalia/frenta/Shutterstock.com; p. 7 Kevin Schafer/age fotostock/Getty Images; p. 8 Yury Kosourov/Shutterstock.com; p. 9 Charles Knowles/Shutterstock.com; p. 10 daulon/Shutterstock.com; p. 11 beboy/Shutterstock.com; p. 12 Jorge Moro/Shutterstock.com; p. 13 (left) photo.ua/Shutterstock.com; p. 13 (right) FeSeven/Shutterstock.com; p. 14 Siim Sepp/Shutterstock.com; p. 15 Doug Meek/Shutterstock.com; p. 16 Microstock Man/Shutterstock.com; p. 17 Marcio Jose Bastos Silva/Shutterstock.com; p. 19 Grant Dixon/Lonely Planet Images/Getty Images; p. 20 Cheryl A. Meyer/Shutterstock.com; p. 21 inacio pires/Shutterstock.com; p. 22 Paul B. Moore/Shutterstock.com.

Publisher's Cataloguing Data

Dee, Willa.
Earth's Rock Cycle / by Willa Dee.
    p. cm. — (Rocks: the hard facts)
Includes index.
ISBN 978-1-4777-2903-8 (library binding) — ISBN 978-1-4777-2992-2 (pbk.) —
ISBN 978-1-4777-3062-1 (6-pack)
1. Petrology — Juvenile literature. 2. Geochemical cycles — Juvenile literature. I. Title.
QE432.2 D44 2014
552—dc23
Manufactured in the United States of America

CPSIA Compliance Information: Batch #W14PK4: For Further Information contact Rosen Publishing, New York, New York at 1-800-237-9932

CONTENTS

ALWAYS CHANGING

The planet Earth is made of **layers**. The outer, or top, layer is the crust. The crust is made of three types of rock. They are **sedimentary rock**, **igneous rock**, and **metamorphic rock**. Each type of rock is formed in a different way. However, each type will slowly change over time from one type to another.

These changes form a **cycle**, called the rock cycle. The rock cycle helps us understand how the **surface** of our Earth was formed. It shows us that Earth is always changing. Go outside and pick up a rock. In a few million years, that rock will have changed!

THE ROCK CYCLE KEY

A - Igneous to Sedimentary
Erosion turns igneous rock to sediment. Pressure fuses sediment together.

B - Sedimentary to Metamorphic
Heat and pressure turn sedimentary rock that is buried underground into metamorphic rock

C - Metamorphic to Igneous
Heat and pressure melt metamorphic rock into magma. Magma cools and hardens into igneous rock.

D - Igneous to Metamorphic
Heat and pressure turn igneous rock that is buried underground into metamorphic rock.

E - Metamorphic to Sedimentary
Erosion turns metamorphic rock into sediment. Pressure fuses sediment together.

F - Sedimentary to Igneous
Heat and pressure melt sedimentary rock into magma. Magma cools and becomes igneous rock.

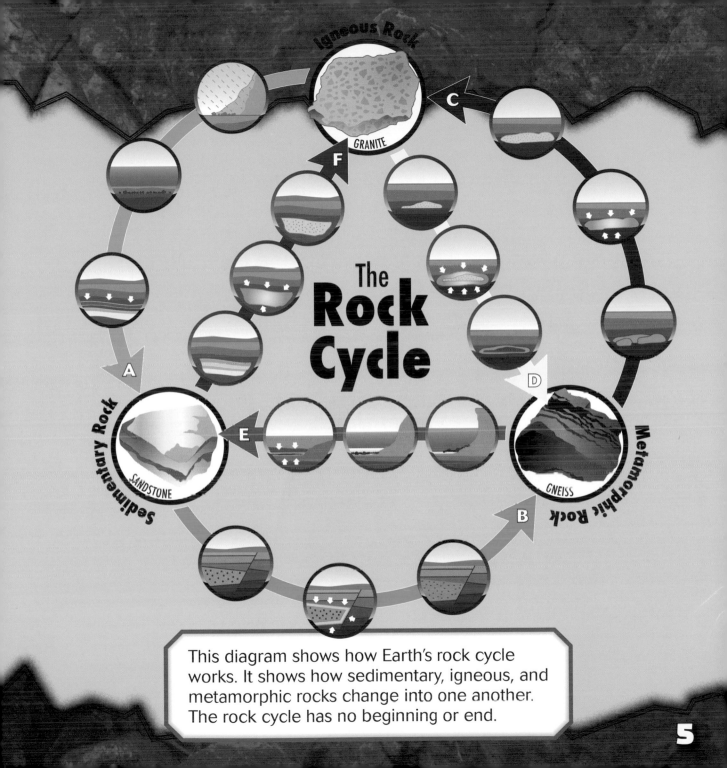

The Rock Cycle

Igneous Rock
GRANITE

Sedimentary Rock
SANDSTONE

Metamorphic Rock
GNEISS

This diagram shows how Earth's rock cycle works. It shows how sedimentary, igneous, and metamorphic rocks change into one another. The rock cycle has no beginning or end.

LAYERS AND PLATES

Earth has different layers. Its center is the core. Above the core is the mantle. The mantle is made up of very hot rock. The rock is so hot it melts into **magma** and flows like a slow-moving river. Next is the outer layer, the crust.

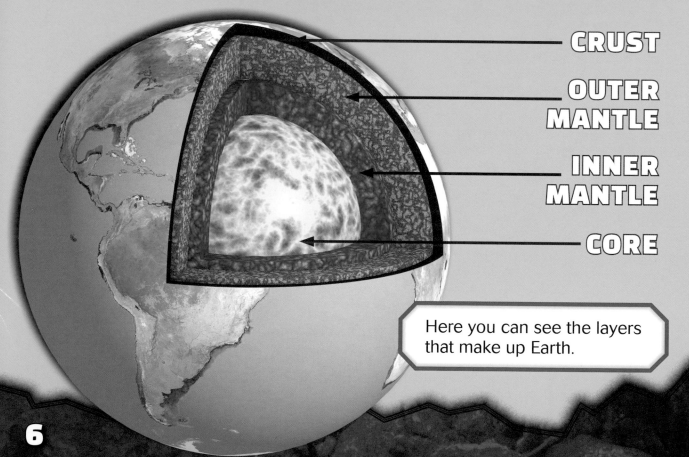

CRUST

OUTER MANTLE

INNER MANTLE

CORE

Here you can see the layers that make up Earth.

This is the San Andreas Fault, in California. A fault line is a break in the ground that happens when Earth's plates move or shift.

Together, rock from the crust and the top of the mantle form large pieces, called plates. These plates float on the lower mantle's flowing magma. They are always moving.

Where two plates meet, rock may be pushed down and become magma. Magma may also cool into solid rock. This heating and cooling of rock is part of the rock cycle.

MINERALS AND CRYSTALS

This is a mineral called feldspar. Feldspar makes up around 60 percent of Earth's crust.

All rocks are made up of **minerals**. Different types of rock are made of different types of minerals. When minerals have a chance to grow in nature, they form **crystals**. This often happens when **liquid** rock flows into cracks underground, leaving minerals behind. In these tight spaces, the minerals can grow and form into crystals. Crystals often have flat edges, and they **reflect** light like tiny mirrors.

Underground, minerals, rocks, and gases are under high heat and **pressure**. These forces cause them to melt together, forming magma. The changes caused by these forces are part of the rock cycle.

Here you can see a white crystal made from quartz. Quartz crystals are found in many colors, such as pink, purple, and yellow.

MAGMA AND VOLCANOES

There is a lot of pressure under Earth's surface. This can cause magma to push up into Earth's crust, which is cooler than the mantle. If the magma cools down enough inside the crust, it hardens. When magma hardens under the surface, it forms igneous rock.

Here you can see magma rising to the top of a volcano and exploding, becoming lava. Ash sprays into the air. Volcanic ash is made of small pieces of rocks and minerals.

VOLCANO

ASH

LAVA

MAGMA

In this picture, a volcano is erupting. Hot lava flows down its sides. Lava can reach 2,200° F (1,200° C)!

When there is too much pressure underground, magma can push through cracks in Earth's crust up to the surface. This is a volcano. Once the magma has reached the outside, it is then called lava. Over time, the lava will cool and harden, forming igneous rock above ground.

IGNEOUS ROCK

There are many ways that igneous rocks form. Each way creates a different kind of rock. Granite is made from magma that has slowly cooled underground. Pumice forms from lava. When lava explodes out of a volcano quickly, the lava gathers gas bubbles. The holes left from the gas bubbles after it has cooled and hardened make pumice very light.

Here you can see igneous rock on the coast of Maine. This rock formed from hardened lava after a volcanic eruption.

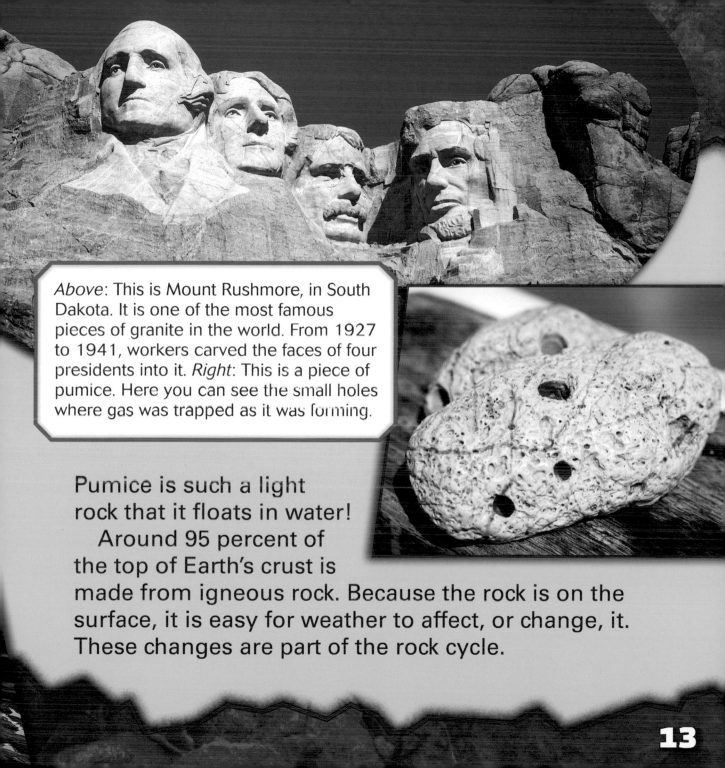

Above: This is Mount Rushmore, in South Dakota. It is one of the most famous pieces of granite in the world. From 1927 to 1941, workers carved the faces of four presidents into it. *Right*: This is a piece of pumice. Here you can see the small holes where gas was trapped as it was forming.

Pumice is such a light rock that it floats in water! Around 95 percent of the top of Earth's crust is made from igneous rock. Because the rock is on the surface, it is easy for weather to affect, or change, it. These changes are part of the rock cycle.

WEATHERING AND EROSION

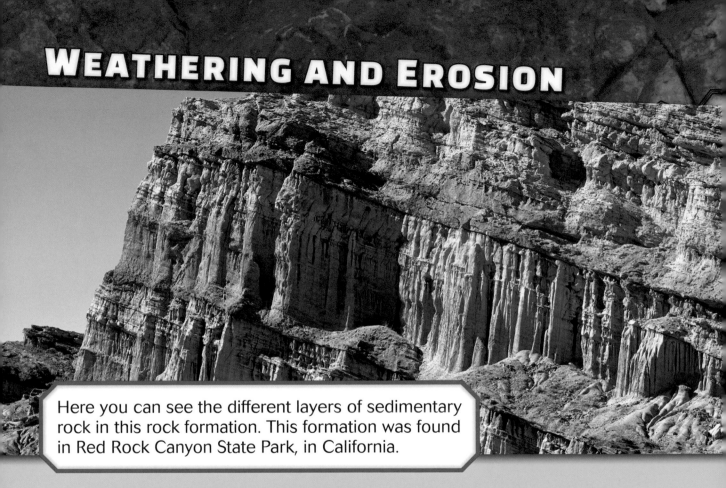

Here you can see the different layers of sedimentary rock in this rock formation. This formation was found in Red Rock Canyon State Park, in California.

Rock may seem very hard. However, wind and rain can slowly wear it down, breaking it into smaller pieces. This process in the rock cycle is called weathering. Erosion is when moving water and ice wear rock down. As the wind or water move during weathering and erosion, they carry away small pieces of rock.

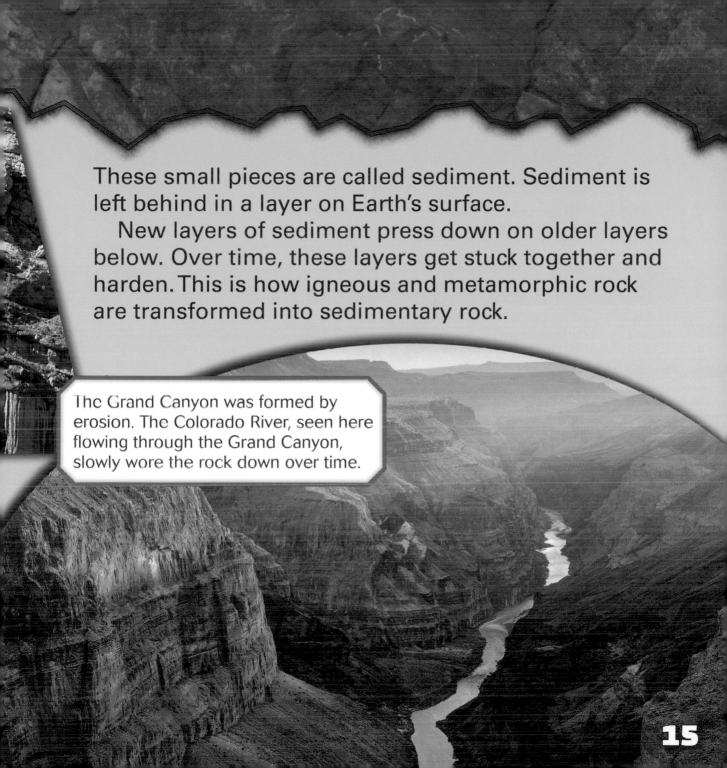

These small pieces are called sediment. Sediment is left behind in a layer on Earth's surface.

New layers of sediment press down on older layers below. Over time, these layers get stuck together and harden. This is how igneous and metamorphic rock are transformed into sedimentary rock.

The Grand Canyon was formed by erosion. The Colorado River, seen here flowing through the Grand Canyon, slowly wore the rock down over time.

SEDIMENTARY ROCK

Sedimentary rock is often found on the bottoms of oceans, lakes, and rivers. Sometimes, plants and animals that have died there are covered by sediment. As the sediment hardens into rock, the plant or animal's remains are trapped.

This is Mount Everest, in Nepal. At 29,029 feet (8,848 m), it is the tallest mountain in the world. Mount Everest is made of sedimentary rock.

This is a fish fossil that was found in sedimentary rock. As the fish rotted, minerals took its place, leaving the shape of the fish behind on the rock.

As the remains rot, minerals take their place. However, the shape of the plant or animal stays and leaves its shape in the rock. This is called a fossil. Most fossils are found in sedimentary rock.

Sedimentary rock can move deep beneath the surface of Earth over time. There, it is under high heat and pressure. This can cause the rock to change.

HEAT AND PRESSURE

Within Earth's crust, the top layers of rock press down on the layers of rock below. This creates pressure as well as heat. Earth's plates, which are always moving against each other, can cause this, too. Nearby magma adds even more heat.

All of this heat and pressure can cause the rock to slowly metamorphose, or change form. Have you ever seen a caterpillar turn into a butterfly? That is called metamorphosis. Just like a caterpillar can change, rocks can change form, too. Rocks that are created through heat and pressure underground are called metamorphic rock.

Gneiss, seen here, is a common type of metamorphic rock. It is made up of mostly quartz and feldspar. Gneiss can be found all over the world.

METAMORPHIC ROCK

Metamorphic rock is often formed from the heat and pressure caused by the plates in Earth's crust rubbing and pushing against each other. This movement of the plates can cause metamorphic rock to rise up. Sometimes, the rock rises high above the land around it. Many **mountain ranges** around the world were made this way.

Wheeler Peak, seen here, is a Nevada mountain made of metamorphic rock. The mountain was formed when Earth's plates came together and pushed the rock upward.

Marble, a type of metamorphic rock, is mined. It is used to make sculptures, counters, and buildings.

On Earth's surface, weathering and erosion can wear down metamorphic rock, which makes sediment. The sediment will get stuck together, becoming sedimentary rock. Metamorphic rock that gets trapped underground is faced with heat, creating magma. When it cools, the magma becomes igneous rock. The rock cycle never ends!

STUDYING THE ROCK CYCLE

Scientists who study Earth's rocks are called geologists. Understanding the rock cycle has helped geologists learn how different rock formations on Earth came to be formed. Studying fossils inside sedimentary rock allows geologists to see the shapes of some of the plants and animals that lived here millions of years ago.

You do not have to be a geologist to study rocks and the rock cycle, though. You can find some of these types of rocks right in your backyard. You will be holding Earth's past in your hands!

This man is studying rocks by breaking them apart with a tool called a rock hammer. Breaking the rocks open will help him learn more about them.

GLOSSARY

crystals (KRIS-tulz) Hard, usually clear, matter that has angles and flat surfaces.

cycle (SY-kul) Actions that happen in the same order over and over.

igneous rock (IG-nee-us ROK) Hot, liquid, underground mineral that has cooled and hardened.

layers (LAY-erz) Thicknesses of things.

liquid (LIH-kwed) Matter that flows.

magma (MAG-muh) A hot, liquid rock underneath Earth's surface.

metamorphic rock (meh-tuh-MOR-fik ROK) Rock that has been changed by heat and pressure.

minerals (MIN-rulz) Natural matter that is not animals, plants, or other living things.

mountain ranges (MOWN-tun RAYNJ-ez) Series of mountains. Two or more mountain ranges together form a mountain system.

pressure (PREH-shur) A force that pushes on something.

reflect (rih-FLEKT) To throw back light, heat, or sound.

sedimentary rock (seh-deh-MEN-teh-ree ROK) Layers of stones, sand, or mud that have been pressed together to form rock.

surface (SER-fes) The outside of anything.

INDEX

WEBSITES

Due to the changing nature of Internet links, PowerKids Press has developed an online list of websites related to the subject of this book. This site is updated regularly. Please use this link to access the list:
www.powerkidslinks.com/rthf/cycle/